Raspberry Pi 5 User Guide

The Complete Guide for Beginners and Experts
Alike to Learn How to Use Your Raspberry Pi 5 for
Everything from Desktop Computing to Robotics

Pearl Davis

Copyright © **Pearl Davis**, 2023

All rights reserved. No part of this publication may be reproduced, distributed, or transmitted in any form or by any means, including photocopying, recording, or any other electronic or mechanical methods, with or without prior written permission of the publisher, except in the case of brief quotations embodied in critical reviews and certain other non-commercial uses permitted by copyright law.

Table of Contents

Introduction

Part 1: Hardware

Part 2: Software

Part 3: Desktop computing

Part 4: Media centre

Part 5: Retro gaming

Part 6: Home automation

Part 7: Education

Part 8: Robotics

Part 9: Industrial Applications

Part 10: Advanced topics

Appendix

Introduction

A compact and reasonably priced computer, the Raspberry Pi may be used for a multitude of tasks, including robotics, media centering, and desktop computing. It's an excellent resource for learning programming and computers, and it's also a lot of fun to use.

Whether you're a novice or an expert, this guide is meant to help you get started with your new Raspberry Pi 5, including:

* How to install and operate software;
* How to configure your Raspberry Pi 5;
* How to use the Raspberry Pi 5 for a variety of purposes, including robotics, media centre, home automation, desktop computing, and retro gaming Solutions for troubleshooting
You can make whatever you can think of with your Raspberry Pi 5. Simple web pages to intricate

robotics are all within the capabilities of the Raspberry Pi 5.

What is a Raspberry Pi?

A Raspberry Pi is a tiny, inexpensive computer with a multitude of applications. Approximately the size of a credit card, it features multiple connections for attaching peripheral devices, like a keyboard, mouse, camera, and monitor.

A single-board computer (SBC), which is a compact circuit board with all of the fundamental parts of a computer, including a CPU, RAM, and storage, powers the Raspberry Pi. Additional GPIO pins on the Raspberry Pi are available for connecting to sensors and other electronic devices.

A fantastic tool for studying computers and programming is the Raspberry Pi. In addition, it is a well-liked option for makers and hobbyists who use it to build their own robots, weather stations, and smart home appliances.

Among the many things you can do with it are:
* Use it as a desktop computer
* Turn it into a media centre to view movies and TV shows
* Construct a vintage game console
* Set up a web server
* Host a Minecraft server
* Build a robot
* Construct a weather station
* Create a home automation system
* And much more!

There are many uses for the Raspberry Pi, which is a cost-effective and adaptable computer. It is an excellent learning tool for makers, enthusiasts, and everyone in between.

Why use a Raspberry Pi?

The Raspberry Pi is useful for a variety of purposes. It's affordable. Especially in comparison to conventional desktop and laptop computers, the Raspberry Pi is a very reasonably priced computer.

It's adaptable. There are several uses for the Raspberry Pi, including robotics, media centering, and desktop computers.

Open source software. Because the Raspberry Pi is built using open source hardware and software, you have total control over your gadget.

A sizable and vibrant Raspberry Pi community exists. This indicates that a wealth of resources are available to assist consumers in getting started and resolving issues.

Utilising the Raspberry Pi is a lot of fun. It's an excellent method to exercise creativity and create original work.

Construct a desktop PC. A desktop PC that is completely functioning can be made with the Raspberry Pi. The Raspberry Pi can run a number of operating systems, such as Windows 10 IoT Core, Ubuntu, and Raspberry Pi OS.

Construct a media centre. You may construct a media centre using a Raspberry Pi to view TV episodes and movies. The Raspberry Pi can run a variety of media centre software programmes, including Plex and Kodi.

Assemble a vintage game system. Classic video games can be played on a retro gaming console that can be configured using a Raspberry Pi. RetroPie and Recalbox are two examples of the many retro gaming software packages that are available for the Raspberry Pi.

Build a system for home automation. You can build a home automation system with the Raspberry Pi to manage your appliances, lighting, and other devices. The Raspberry Pi can run several home automation software programmes, including OpenHAB and Home Assistant.

Construct a robot. One can construct a robot with the Raspberry Pi. Numerous robotic platforms are available for the Raspberry Pi, including the PiBorg PirateBot and the Raspberry Pi 3 Model B+ Robot Kit.

Establish a weather station. A weather station that tracks temperature, humidity, and other meteorological parameters can be built with a Raspberry Pi. WeeWX and Cumulus MX are two of the several weather station software programmes that are available for the Raspberry Pi.

Configure your web server. You may use the Raspberry Pi to build up a web server and run your own blog or website. Numerous web server software programmes, including Apache and Nginx, are available for the Raspberry Pi.

Running a server for Minecraft. In order to play Minecraft with your buddies, you can utilise the Raspberry Pi to host a server. For the Raspberry Pi, several Minecraft server software programmes are available, including Spigot and PaperMC.

Some specific examples of how people use Raspberry Pi

Students: In order to learn about computers and programming, students use Raspberry Pis. They construct projects for their classmates using them as well.

Hobbyists: With Raspberry Pis, hobbyists can construct a wide range of projects, including robots, weather stations, and smart home appliances.

Makers: To prototype and produce new goods, makers utilise Raspberry Pis.

Companies: Companies run their servers and web pages on Raspberry Pis. They also make advantage of them to craft unique answers to their own problems.

Getting started with your Raspberry Pi 5

Getting started with your Raspberry Pi 5 is easy. Just follow these steps:

1. Gather your supplies: You will need the following:

   * Raspberry Pi 5
   * MicroSD card (at least 8GB)
   * Power supply (5V 3A)
   * HDMI cable
   * Monitor

* Keyboard

* Mouse

2. Set up the OS for Raspberry Pi: Visit the Raspberry Pi website to download the most recent version of Raspberry Pi OS. With an application such as Raspberry Pi Imager, write the image to your microSD card.

3. Connect your Raspberry Pi: Attach your Raspberry Pi to the power supply, HDMI cable, monitor, keyboard, and mouse.

4. Start up your Raspberry Pi: Place the microSD card and power supply into your Raspberry Pi. After your Raspberry Pi has finished booting up, the desktop will appear.

5. Follow the directions on the screen: The Raspberry Pi desktop will guide you through the

initial setup steps, including setting up a network connection and creating a user account.

You are now prepared to use your Raspberry Pi 5! Just finish the setup process!

Part 1: Hardware

Overview of Raspberry Pi 5 hardware

The Raspberry Pi Foundation in the UK is responsible for developing the Raspberry Pi 5, a single-board computer. On September 28, 2023, the Raspberry Pi 5th generation was made available.

The Raspberry Pi 5 has a VideoCore VII GPU and a quad-core Broadcom BCM2712 Arm Cortex-A76 processor running at 2.4GHz. There are two RAM configurations available: 4GB and 8GB.

Numerous ports and connectors are available on the Raspberry Pi 5, these include:
* Gigabit Ethernet port
* HDMI port
* MicroSD card slot
* GPIO connector
* Power connector

* 2 × 4-lane MIPI camera/display transceivers
* PCI Express 2.0 x1 interface for quick peripherals
* 2 × USB 3.0 ports
* 2 × USB 2.0 ports
* Gigabit Ethernet port
* 3.5mm audio jack
* MicroSD card slot.

Raspberry Pi 5 hardware specifications

Specification	Value
CPU	Broadcom BCM2712 quad-core Arm Cortex-A76 @ 2.4GHz
GPU	VideoCore VII
RAM	4GB or 8GB LPDDR4X-4267
Storage	MicroSD card
Display output	Dual 4Kp60 HDMI with HDR support
Audio output	3.5mm audio jack
Network	Gigabit Ethernet
USB ports	2 × USB 3.0, 2 × USB 2.0

Other ports	PCI Express 2.0 x1, 2 × 4-lane MIPI camera/display transceivers, microSD card slot, power port
Power supply	5V 3A
Dimensions	85.60 × 56.50 × 21.00 mm
Weight	45g

Configuring the Raspberry Pi 5

What you'll need to set up your Raspberry Pi 5: HDMI cable, Power source (5V/3A), Raspberry Pi 5, MicroSD card (at least 8GB), monitor, keyboard, and mouse.

Actions:
1. Connect your computer to the microSD card.
2. Visit the Raspberry Pi website to download the most recent Raspberry Pi OS version.
3. Use an application such as Raspberry Pi Imager to write the image to the microSD card.
4. Put the Raspberry Pi's microSD card inside.

5. Attach your Raspberry Pi to the power source, HDMI cable, monitor, keyboard, and mouse.

6. Attach the power source to an electrical outlet.

After your Raspberry Pi has finished booting up, the desktop will appear.

Linking accessories

A multitude of peripherals can be connected to your Raspberry Pi 5, such as:

Screens: Your Raspberry Pi 5 supports up to two HDMI-connected screens. HDR output is also supported by the Raspberry Pi 5.

USB gadgets: Your Raspberry Pi 5 can be connected to a wide range of USB peripherals, such as external storage devices, webcams, mice, and keyboards. There are two USB 3.0 and two USB 2.0 ports on the Raspberry Pi 5.

Network: You can use Ethernet or WiFi to link your Raspberry Pi 5 to a network. The Raspberry Pi 5 can support dual-band 802.11ac WiFi and features a gigabit Ethernet connector.

Camera: The Raspberry Pi 5's MIPI camera connector allows you to attach a camera to the device. Numerous camera modules, such as the Raspberry Pi Camera Module V2 and the Raspberry Pi Camera Module 3, are compatible with the Raspberry Pi 5.

Additional accessories: Using the GPIO pins on your Raspberry Pi 5, you may easily attach other peripherals. You can attach sensors, actuators, and other electronic devices to the GPIO pins.

Simply insert the peripheral into the designated port to connect it to your Raspberry Pi 5. For instance, you would insert the HDMI wire from the monitor into the Raspberry Pi 5's HDMI port to attach a display to the device.

After attaching a peripheral to your Raspberry Pi 5, you might have to install extra drivers or software.

For instance, you must install the Raspberry Pi Camera Software if you want to attach a camera to your Raspberry Pi 5.

The following tips will help you connect peripherals to your Raspberry Pi 5

Make use of premium cables. This will support maintaining a dependable connection.

Verify that the Raspberry Pi 5 can interface with the peripherals you use.

Verify that the USB device you are connecting is formatted for Linux.

You could try rebooting your Raspberry Pi 5 if you are experiencing issues attaching a device.

Troubleshoot hardware issues

The following advice will help you troubleshoot hardware issues with your Raspberry Pi 5:

Check the electricity source: Verify that the Raspberry Pi 5 is receiving enough power from the power source and that it is connected correctly. A 5V/3A power supply is needed for the Raspberry Pi 5.

Check the microSD card: Verify that the microSD card is compatible with the Raspberry Pi 5 and that it has been inserted correctly. To find out if the microSD card is corrupt, you can use a programme like Raspberry Pi Imager.

Check the wires: Verify that all of the cables are securely fastened and free of damage.

Another port to try: If a specific peripheral is giving you problems, consider attaching it to a different port. For instance, attempt attaching a USB keyboard to a different USB port if you are experiencing issues with it.

Upgrade the OS on your Raspberry Pi: Verify the operating system on your Raspberry Pi is current. New features and security updates are frequently added to the Raspberry Pi OS. To guarantee the greatest experience, it's critical to maintain your Raspberry Pi OS updated.

Verify the documentation for the Raspberry Pi: The documentation for the Raspberry Pi is an excellent tool for diagnosing hardware issues. Numerous articles and tutorials on troubleshooting common hardware issues are included in the documentation.

Seek assistance: In case you need assistance with resolving a hardware issue, you can reach out to additional online resources like the Raspberry Pi forums.

The following are detailed troubleshooting guidelines for typical hardware issues:

The Raspberry Pi 5 won't turn on

Check the microSD card, the power supply, and try an alternative port.

Your Raspberry Pi OS needs an update.

The Raspberry Pi 5 is sluggish

* Upgrade your Raspberry Pi's operating system.

* Use a faster microSD card.

* Increase the Raspberry Pi 5's speed.

The Raspberry Pi 5 is becoming too hot

* Give your Raspberry Pi 5 a heatsink.

* Cool your Raspberry Pi 5 with a fan.

* Reduce the speed of your Raspberry Pi 5.

Unable to connect Raspberry Pi 5 to a network

* Examine the network wire

* Verify the network configuration

* Your Raspberry Pi OS needs an update.

USB device not recognised by Raspberry Pi 5

Verify that the USB device is formatted for Linux

Try a different port.

Your Raspberry Pi OS needs an update.

Part 2: Software

Raspberry Pi OS overview

For use with the Raspberry Pi line of single-board computers, Raspberry Pi OS is an operating system based on Debian. The Raspberry Pi Foundation is responsible for developing this official operating system for the Raspberry Pi.

An efficient and light-weight operating system that is tailored for the Raspberry Pi's hardware is called Raspberry Pi OS. Numerous pre-installed applications are included, including a text editor, file manager, and web browser. Additional applications can be installed from the Raspberry Pi applications Centre as well.

Overview of the main features of Raspberry Pi OS

Debian-based: The popular Linux distribution Debian serves as the foundation for Raspberry Pi

OS. This indicates that a large selection of applications and support are available to you.

Compact and effective: The Raspberry Pi OS is tailored to the Raspberry Pi's specifications.

Pre-installed software: Raspberry Pi OS comes with a range of pre-installed software, such as a web browser, file organiser, and text editor. This makes it an excellent choice for even the most basic Raspberry Pi models. This implies that you can immediately begin using your Raspberry Pi.

Raspberry Pi Software Centre: This resource gives you quick access to a variety of applications that you can set up on your Raspberry Pi. Open source and free: Raspberry Pi OS is open source and free. This implies that you can change the code to suit your needs and use it for any purpose.

Installing and using software

You can follow these instructions to install and utilise applications on your Raspberry Pi 5:

1. Launch the software centre for the Raspberry Pi.
2. Look through or perform a search for the installation programme.
3. Select the software by clicking the Install option.
4. Await the software's installation.
5. You can use the Raspberry Pi desktop to launch the software after it has been installed.

Software can also be installed via the command line. To accomplish this, launch a terminal window and go to the software's directory. Next, execute the subsequent command:

"**sudo apt install <software_name>**"

For instance, you may use the following command to install the Apache web server:

sudo apt install apache2

The software can be launched after installation by using the following command:

Sudo service <software_name> start

26

For instance, you would use the following command to launch the Apache web server:

'Subduo service apache2 start'

Software can also be removed via the command line or the Raspberry Pi Software Centre. Software can be removed from the Raspberry Pi Software Centre by right-clicking on it and choosing Remove. Use the following command to uninstall applications from the command line:

"sudo apt remove \software_name>"

For instance, you would use the following command to remove the Apache web server:

"sudo apt uninstall apache2"

Tips to set up and operate applications on your Raspberry Pi 5

Verify that you are connected to the internet. The majority of software need an online download in order to be installed. Verify that your microSD card has adequate free space.

27

Software packages might vary greatly in size. Take care not to misspell the software name while installing it via the command line. This could harm your Raspberry Pi 5 or lead to the incorrect software being installed. You can get assistance from other online resources like the Raspberry Pi forums if you are having problems installing or using software.

Software Management

You will need to manage your Raspberry Pi 5 after installing some applications. This covers backing up, updating, and uninstalling your programme.

Upgrading your programme

Keeping your software updated is crucial. Performance enhancements and security patches are frequently included in software upgrades. You can use the command line or the Raspberry Pi Software Centre to update your software.

Open the Raspberry Pi Software Centre and select the Updates option to upgrade your software using that tool. Next to each update, select the Install Now button.

Open a terminal window and type the following command to update your software via the command line:

"sudo apt upgrade and sudo apt update:

Using this command, your Raspberry Pi 5's software packages will all be updated.

Software uninstalling

You can free up space on your microSD card by uninstalling software that you are no longer using. You can use the command line or the Raspberry Pi Software Centre to remove software.

Using the Raspberry Pi Software Centre, right-click the programme and choose Remove to uninstall it.

29

To use the command line to uninstall software, launch a terminal window and type the following command:

"sudo apt remove \software_name>"

Enter the name of the programme you wish to remove in place of {<software_name>}.

Creating a software backup

Regularly backing up your software is essential. This will safeguard your software from corrupted or lost data. There are several ways you can backup your software, including:

Compressing your programme directory and saving it on an external device or cloud storage service

Making a microSD card clone and transferring it to a new microSD card.

Employing a specialised backup programme, such Deja Dup or rsync.

Software Troubleshooting

Problems can occasionally arise with even the best software. There are several steps you may take to debug software if you are experiencing issues with it:

Restart your Raspberry Pi 5 — This frequently resolves little issues.

Check for updates: Bug fixes are frequently included in software upgrades.

Experiment with a different software version. Try updating to a newer version of the software if you are currently using an older one.

Please refer to the software's documentation. There may be troubleshooting information on common issues in the software documentation.

Look up assistance online: You can solve software issues with the aid of a plethora of web tools. You can post a question on the Raspberry Pi forums or in other online groups if you are still having issues.

Describe the issue precisely: The more details you can give, the simpler it will be for someone to assist you.

Make an effort to duplicate the issue: Troubleshooting will be simpler if the issue can be consistently reproduced.

Disable any superfluous software: Try disabling any other software that you are not using if the issue is limited to a certain software programme. This may aid in focusing the issue.

Please attempt to boot your Raspberry Pi 5 in Safe Mode. Your Raspberry Pi 5 boots into Safe Mode with just the most necessary apps running. When debugging issues brought on by third-party applications, this can be useful.

Part 3: Desktop computing

Using a desktop computer with a Raspberry Pi 5

One potent single-board computer that doubles as a desktop is the Raspberry Pi 5. It is a fantastic option for those looking for an affordable, energy-efficient desktop computer or one that is simple to customise.

Installing and using desktop applications

Numerous pre-installed desktop software, including a web browser, file manager, and text editor, are included with the Raspberry Pi 5. Additional desktop apps can also be installed using the command line via the Raspberry Pi Software Centre.

Open the Raspberry Pi Software Centre and browse or search for the desktop application you wish to install in order to install it. Next, select the application and click the Install option.

Open a terminal window and go to the directory containing the desktop application to install it using the command line. Next, execute the subsequent command:

"sudo apt install <application_name>"

For instance, you may use the following command to install the LibreOffice office suite:

"sudo apt install libreoffice"

You can use the Raspberry Pi desktop to start the application after it has been installed.

Setting up your desktop software

Pre-installed on the Raspberry Pi 5 is the Xfce desktop system. For the Raspberry Pi 5, Xfce is a fast and light desktop environment that works wonderfully.

The Xfce desktop environment is configurable to meet your needs. You can rearrange panels, add new widgets, and alter the wallpaper, for instance. Additional desktop themes and icons can be installed via the command line or the Raspberry Pi Software Centre.

Launch the Settings app to set up the Xfce desktop environment. You may customise every element of the Xfce desktop environment, including the panels, background, and widgets, with the Settings application.

Tips to use the Raspberry Pi 5 as a desktop computer

Opt for a quick microSD card. Your desktop Raspberry Pi 5 computer's performance will be enhanced by a fast microSD card.

Attach a keyboard and monitor. For your desktop Raspberry Pi 5 computer to function, you will require a keyboard and monitor.

Install extra desktop programmes. Additional desktop apps can be installed via the command line via the Raspberry Pi Software Centre.

Set up your desktop settings. The Xfce desktop environment is configurable to meet your needs.

Update your programme frequently. Maintaining the most recent version of your software is essential for optimal performance and security.

Linking up monitor, keyboard, and mouse

You will need the following cables in order to connect your Raspberry Pi 5 to a monitor, keyboard, and mouse:

* A USB cable to connect the mouse;
 * An HDMI cable to connect the display
* A USB cable to connect the keyboard.

After obtaining the required cables, attach the keyboard, mouse, and monitor to the appropriate Raspberry Pi 5 ports.

Web browsing, video watching, and music listening

A web browser, such Chromium, is pre-installed on the Raspberry Pi 5. To navigate the internet, just use your web browser and type in the URL of the desired website.

You can use the built-in video player, like VLC Media Player, to watch videos. Just launch the video player and select the desired video file to begin playing.

You can use the built-in audio player, like Clementine, to listen to music. Just launch the audio player and navigate to the desired music file to start playing it.

Using software for productivity

An office suite, such LibreOffice, is pre-installed on the Raspberry Pi 5. Open one of the applications, like LibreOffice Writer or LibreOffice Calc, to begin using the office suite.

Additional productivity apps can also be installed via the command line via the Raspberry Pi apps Centre. For instance, you would issue the following command to install the GIMP image editor:

'sudo apt install gimp'

The productivity programme can be launched from the Raspberry Pi desktop once it has been installed.

Utilising the Raspberry Pi 5 for gaming

You can play a lot of different games on the powerful single-board computer that is the Raspberry Pi 5. You can play both contemporary games like Counter-Strike: Global Offensive and Minecraft, as well as classic classics like Super Mario Bros. and Sonic the Hedgehog.

You must install a game emulator or game engine on the Raspberry Pi 5 in order to play games on it. You may use your Raspberry Pi 5 to play games from earlier consoles by using a game emulator. A software development environment that lets you make and play games is called a game engine.

For the Raspberry Pi 5, try these well-liked game engines and emulators
Video game engines: Unreal Engine, Godot, Unity
Game emulators: RetroPie, Recalbox, Lakka

You can install games after setting up a game engine or emulator. Installing games is possible via the command line, the Raspberry Pi Software Centre, and internet resources.

Open the Raspberry Pi Software Centre, navigate, or do a search for the game you wish to install in order to install it. Next, select the game and click the Install option.

Open a terminal window and go to the directory containing the game to install it using the command line. Next, execute the subsequent command:

sudo apt install <game_name>

Put the name of the game you wish to install in lieu of **<game_name>**

You must first download the game file from the internet and transfer it to your Raspberry Pi 5 in order to install it. Once the game file is on your Raspberry Pi 5, run the following command to install it:

sudo apt install <game_file_name>

Replace <game_file_name> with the name of the game file.

You can use the Raspberry Pi desktop to start the game after it has been installed.

Tips for using the Raspberry Pi 5 to play games
Make use of a remote. Using a controller with your Raspberry Pi 5 will simplify gaming.

Attach your HDTV to your Raspberry Pi 5. You'll have an improved gaming experience as a result.

Increase the Raspberry Pi 5's speed. Your Raspberry Pi 5's performance will increase with overclocking, which is advantageous while playing demanding games.

Troubleshooting Raspberry Pi 5 desktop issues

There are several things you can attempt to troubleshoot issues with your Raspberry Pi 5 desktop if you are experiencing them:

Restart your Raspberry Pi 5 — This frequently resolves little issues.

Check for updates: Bug fixes are frequently included in software upgrades.

Experiment with an alternative desktop setup:If you are using the Xfce desktop environment by default, consider installing and utilising GNOME or LXDE as an alternative desktop environment.

Verify the documentation for the Raspberry Pi: You may find information about troubleshooting specific desktop issues in the Raspberry Pi documentation.

Look up assistance online: You can solve Raspberry Pi desktop issues with a plethora of web resources.

Part 4: Media centre

Using Raspberry Pi 5 as a media centre

Playing music and video files on your TV is possible with a media centre. A media centre can also be used to view streaming video services like Hulu and Netflix.

A powerful and adaptable single-board computer that can be used as a media centre is the Raspberry Pi 5. It's a terrific option for those looking for an affordable, energy-efficient media centre or one that's simple to customise.

Installing and using media centre applications

The Raspberry Pi 5 has access to numerous media centre applications. Several well-liked media centre programmes include of:

* Plex
* OSMC
* LibreELEC
* Kodi

Using a tool like Raspberry Pi Imager, you can download the image file from the media centre application's website and then write it to a microSD card to install it on the Raspberry Pi 5. You can put the microSD card into your Raspberry Pi 5 and boot it up after the image file has been written to it.

You can use the media centre programme to play audio and video files as soon as it boots up. The media centre application allows you to watch streaming video content as well.

Configuring your media centre

You can begin setting your Raspberry Pi 5 media centre application after installing it. The media centre application you are using will determine which configuration choices apply to it.

Nonetheless, the majority of media centre programmes let you set up the following:

* Network settings
* Add-ons
* Streaming video services
 * Video and audio settings

Navigate to the settings menu to configure your media centre. All of your media centre's configuration options are available through the settings menu.

Tips on how to use the Raspberry Pi 5 as a media centre

Make use of an excellent HDMI cable. You'll receive the highest quality video possible if you do this.
 Use an Ethernet wire to link your Raspberry Pi 5 to your television. Compared to Wi-Fi, this will offer a quicker and more dependable connection.

Make use of a cordless remote. You will be able to operate your media centre from the comfort of your couch thanks to this.

Apply a skin to your media centre. Your media centre's appearance and feel can be altered with a media centre skin.

Put in add-ons. Your media centre's capabilities can be increased with add-ons. Installing add-ons, for instance, allows you to play new media file formats and watch new streaming video services.

Playing movies, music, and TV shows

To utilise your Raspberry Pi 5 media centre for watching films, music, and TV shows, you can:

* Put the media files on an external hard drive or microSD card, then attach it to your Raspberry Pi 5.

* Stream the media files from another computer on your network or from a network attached storage (NAS) device.

* Play the media files via an internet provider, such Hulu or Netflix.

To enjoy films, songs, and TV series from an external hard drive or microSD card, just launch the media centre app and go to the media files. After that, choose the media file to play and press the Play button.

In order to stream media content—such as movies, music, and TV shows—from a networked PC or NAS device, you must first add the network share to your media centre programme. You can navigate to the network share and play the media files when it has been added.

For your media centre application, you must install a streaming video service plugin in order to play movies, music, and TV shows from an internet service. You can play movies, music, and TV series

47

after installing the plugin and logging into your streaming video account.

Streaming media from the internet

The Raspberry Pi 5 media centre is compatible with a wide range of streaming video services. Among the well-known streaming video services are:

* Disney+
* HBO Max
* Netflix
* Hulu
* Amazon Prime Video
* YouTube TV

Installing a streaming video service plugin for your media centre application is necessary in order to stream media from an online service. You can play movies, music, and TV series after installing the plugin and logging into your streaming video account.

Watching live TV and recording it

You may record and watch live TV with your Raspberry Pi 5 media centre. A TV antenna and a TV tuner card are required for this.

You can install a live TV recording and playback app, such as tvheadend or MythTV, once you've linked your Raspberry Pi 5 to the TV tuner card and TV antenna. You can start recording and watching live TV as soon as the application is installed and has finished searching for channels.

Troubleshooting media centre problems

Restart your Raspberry Pi 5: This frequently resolves little issues.

Review the Raspberry Pi documentation: There may be troubleshooting instructions for some media centre issues in the documentation.

Look up assistance online: You can solve Raspberry Pi media centre issues with a variety of internet resources.

Verify your media center's configuration: Verify that your media centre is set up properly.

Update the software in your media centre: Updates frequently contain problem fixes.

Experiment with an alternative media centre app: Try installing and utilising a new media centre programme, like OSMC or LibreELEC, if you are already using one of the most widely used ones, like Kodi or Plex.

* Verify the hardware you have. Verify that the media centre programme is compatible with the hardware you have. For instance, confirm that your Raspberry Pi 5 has the hardware codecs required to play the video file if you are experiencing problems playing it.

In case you are still facing difficulties debugging your media centre issue, you can seek assistance from various online communities like the Raspberry Pi forums.

The following are detailed troubleshooting guidelines for typical media centre issues:

* The media centre freezes or crashes. Restarting your Raspberry Pi 5 might help. Try updating your media centre software if the issue continues. Try installing and using a new media centre application if you are still experiencing issues.

* Some music or video files won't play in Media Centre. Verify that the hardware codecs your Raspberry Pi 5 needs to play the file are installed. The following command can be used to verify this in a terminal window:
"**sudo apt install <codec_name>**"

Change {\codec_name>} to the name of the required codec. You can attempt to convert the file to an alternative format if the codec is not available.

* A streaming video service cannot be connected to via the media centre. Verify that the streaming video service plugin for your media centre application is installed correctly. Try logging back into your streaming video account after the plugin has been installed. Try using a different device to connect to the streaming video service if you are still having issues.

* Live TV cannot be recorded by the media centre. Verify that your Raspberry Pi 5 and TV tuner card are properly connected. The following command can be used to verify this in a terminal window:
"tvheadend -t"
A list of every TV channel that your TV tuner card is capable of detecting will appear as a result. Try connecting your TV tuner card to a different USB

port on your Raspberry Pi 5 if it isn't being identified.

If you are still experiencing difficulties troubleshooting your media centre issue, kindly share additional details about the issue, including the media centre application you are using, its version, and the troubleshooting steps you have already performed.

Part 5: Retro gaming

Retro gaming with a Raspberry Pi 5

Retro gaming is a terrific fit for the Raspberry Pi 5. It is reasonably priced and powerful enough to replicate many different old systems.

Installing a vintage gaming programme is required before you can begin playing retro games on the Raspberry Pi 5. Several well-liked retro gaming apps consist of:

* Lakka
* RetroPie
* Recalbox
* Batocera.linux

You must download and install the ROMs for the games you wish to play after installing a retro gaming application. Video game cartridge digital copies are known as ROMs. Online, ROMs can be found; however, take care to only download files from reliable sites.

You must transfer the ROMs to your Raspberry Pi 5 after downloading them. To accomplish this, transfer the ROMs to an external hard drive or microSD card, then attach it to your Raspberry Pi 5.

After the ROMs are installed on your Raspberry Pi 5, launch the retro gaming app, and navigate to the ROMs to begin playing games. Next, choose the ROM you wish to play, then press the Play button.

Tips for playing classic video games on the Raspberry Pi 5

* Make use of an excellent HDMI cable. You'll receive the highest quality video possible if you do this.

Use an Ethernet wire to link your Raspberry Pi 5 to your television. Compared to Wi-Fi, this will offer a quicker and more dependable connection.

Make use of a cordless remote. This will let you play your old-school video game console from the comfort of your couch.

Update the software for your retro games. Bug fixes and new features are frequently included in software updates.

Put in add-ons. Your retro gaming system's capabilities can be increased with add-ons. Installing add-ons, for instance, can enable you to play new games and enhance the functionality of your retro gaming system.

Connecting a controller

You have two options for connecting a controller to your Raspberry Pi 5 retro gaming system: wirelessly or with a USB cable.

Simply insert the USB cord into the Raspberry Pi 5 to connect a controller. The controller will find and set itself automatically.

You must install a wireless controller driver in order to connect a controller via a wireless connection. Wireless controller drivers are included in the majority of vintage gaming apps. After installing the driver, connect your wireless controller by following the guidelines the retro gaming application provides.

Using your TV to play retro games

You must use an HDMI cable to connect your Raspberry Pi 5 to your TV in order to play retro games on it.

You may launch the retro gaming programme and navigate to the ROMs to begin playing games on the Raspberry Pi 5 once it is connected to your TV. Next, choose the ROM you wish to play, then press the Play button.

The majority of retro gaming apps let you adjust the audio and visual configurations. The controls and game parameters are also customizable.

Configuring your retro gaming system

You can begin configuring your Raspberry Pi 5 once you have installed an old-school gaming programme. Depending on which retro gaming software you're using, different setup choices will be available. On the other hand, the majority of vintage gaming apps let you customise the following:

* Network settings
* Game settings
* Input options
* Video and audio settings

Navigate to the options section to customise your retro gaming system. All of your retro gaming system's configuration options are available through the settings menu.

Tips to set up your retro gaming system

* Tailor the controls to your preferences. You may map the controls to any button on your controller with the majority of vintage gaming apps.
* Turn on shaders. Retro games can look better with shaders.
* Permit cheating. Vintage game play can be facilitated by cheats.
* Keep your games saved. You can save your games on most retro gaming apps so you can play them again at a later time.

Troubleshooting retro gaming problems

* Restart your Raspberry Pi 5
* Review the Raspberry Pi documentation: There may be troubleshooting guides available there that address particular issues with retro gaming.

*Look up assistance online: You can solve Raspberry Pi vintage gaming issues using a plethora of web resources.

*Verify your retro gaming system's configuration: Verify the configuration of your retro gaming system. Verify, for instance, that the audio and video settings are set appropriately and that the controls are mapped correctly.

*Update the software for your retro games: Software upgrades frequently come with performance boosts and problem fixes.

* Experiment with an alternative retro gaming app: Try installing and running a new retro gaming programme, such Batocera.linux or Lakka, if you are already using one of the most well-known ones, like RetroPie or Recalbox.

* Verify the hardware you have: Verify that the retro gaming app you're using is compatible with your hardware. Make sure your Raspberry Pi 5 has the required hardware codecs, for instance, if you are experiencing problems playing a specific old game.

You can seek assistance from other online communities like the Raspberry Pi forums if you are still having problems with your retro gaming issue.

For common issues with vintage games, consider the following particular troubleshooting tips:

Antiquated gaming software freezes or crashes. Restarting your Raspberry Pi 5 might help. Update your retro gaming software if the issue continues. Try installing and using an alternative vintage gaming application if you are still experiencing issues.

* **A certain vintage game won't play on a retro gaming application.** To play the game, confirm that your Raspberry Pi 5 has the required hardware codecs. The following command can be used to verify this in a terminal window:

lshw -C display

A list of all the hardware codecs that your Raspberry Pi 5 supports will appear as a result. The game must be converted to a different format if the codec you want is not supported.

The retro gaming software is unable to establish a controller connection. Verify that your Raspberry Pi 5 and controller are connected correctly. Make sure your wireless controller is paired with your Raspberry Pi 5 if you're using one. The following command can be used to verify this in a terminal window:

bluetoothctl

The Bluetooth command-line interface will open as a result. To view a list of every Bluetooth device that is associated, enter the following command:

devices

The result of this command will list your controller if it is associated with your Raspberry Pi 5.

* **The retro gaming software isn't saving my games.** Verify that the settings of the retro gaming application have game saving enabled. Another option is to attempt transferring the game save files to an external hard drive or another location.

The performance of the retro gaming application is subpar. Reduce the audio and visual settings, if possible. Another option is to turn off shaders and other elements that can put a strain on the hardware of your Raspberry Pi 5.

If you are experiencing difficulties troubleshooting your retro gaming issue, kindly share additional details about the issue, including the retro gaming application you are utilising, its version, the retro game you are attempting to play, and the troubleshooting steps you have already performed.

Part 6: Home automation

Using Home Automation with Raspberry Pi 5

An excellent platform for home automation is the Raspberry Pi 5. It is reasonably priced and strong enough to perform a wide range of home automation applications.

Installing a home automation application is a must for beginning home automation on the Raspberry Pi 5. Among the widely used uses for home automation are:

* OpenHAB
* Domoticz
* Node-RED
* Home Assistant

An application for home automation must be configured to connect to your smart home devices after it has been installed. The application you use for home automation will determine how to configure it. Nonetheless, the majority of home automation programmes let you to up the following:

* Devices: Configure and add smart home appliances.
* Automations: Establish rules that cause activities to be taken in response to certain events, such time, place, or device status.
* Dashboards: To monitor and manage the state of your smart home appliances, create dashboards.

You can begin automating your house as soon as your system is configured for home automation. You can set up an automation to, for instance, switch on the lights when you get home or turn off the thermostat when you leave.

Tips for using the Raspberry Pi 5 for home automation

* Make use of a good power supply. This will guarantee dependable operation of your Raspberry Pi 5 at all times.

* Use an Ethernet wire to connect your Raspberry Pi 5 to your network. Compared to Wi-Fi, this will offer a quicker and more dependable connection.

*Update the software for your home automation system. Bug fixes and new features are frequently included in software updates.

*Put in add-ons. Your home automation system's capabilities can be increased with add-ons. To construct additional automations or to support new smart home devices, for instance, you can install add-ons.

Fixing issues with home automation

There are several steps you may take to troubleshoot your home automation system if you're experiencing issues:

* Give your Raspberry Pi 5 a restart. This frequently solves small issues.
* Examine your home automation application's logs. The logs might have details on the issue.
* Look up assistance online. You can solve issues with home automation with a lot of web resources.
* Examine how your home automation system is configured. Verify the configuration of your home automation system.
* Upgrade the software used for home automation. Bug patches are often included in software updates.

You might seek assistance from other online communities or the forums of your home automation application if you are still having difficulties diagnosing the issue.

The following are some particular troubleshooting guidelines for typical issues with home automation:

*Apps for home automation freeze or crash: Restarting your Raspberry Pi 5 might help. Try updating your home automation software if the issue continues. Try installing and utilising a new home automation app if you are still having issues.

*Smart home device not connecting to home automation application: Verify that your smart home device is linked to your network correctly. Restarting your smart home gadget is another option.

*Apps for home automation won't start an automation: Verify that the automation is set up properly. Restarting your Raspberry Pi 5 is an additional option.

The performance of the home automation application is subpar. Try adjusting your home automation app's settings. Another option is to turn off unused add-ons.

If troubleshooting the issue is still proving to be difficult, kindly share additional details about the issue, including the smart home device you are experiencing issues with, the home automation application you are using, its version, and the troubleshooting steps you have already performed.

Part 7: Education

The Raspberry Pi 5 is an excellent educational platform. It is reasonably priced and strong enough to run a wide range of educational applications.

The Raspberry Pi 5 can be used in the following ways in education

Teaching Computer science and programming

Students of all ages can learn programming and computer science using the Raspberry Pi 5. A multitude of instructional resources, including books, online courses, and tutorials, are at one's disposal.

You can teach students on the following topic using the Raspberry Pi 5:

* Operating systems, databases, networking, computer architecture, machine learning, and programming languages like Python and Scratch

Using the Raspberry Pi 5 to build educational projects

Numerous educational projects can be constructed with the Raspberry Pi 5. You may construct the following projects, for instance:

A game console, a music player, a robot, a home automation system, a weather station, and a security system

Students can study a lot of subjects via these projects, including computer science, electronics, and programming.

Teaching students using the Raspberry Pi 5

Teaching a range of courses in the classroom, including physics, maths, computer science, and engineering, is possible with the Raspberry Pi 5.

For instance, you can instruct students on the following subjects using the Raspberry Pi 5:

* You can instruct students in computer science, robotics, and artificial intelligence using the Raspberry Pi 5. The Raspberry Pi 5 can be used to instruct students in maths about data analysis, statistics, and machine learning.
* You can teach biology, chemistry, and physics to students using the Raspberry Pi 5. The Raspberry Pi 5 can be used to instruct students in electronics, mechanics, and design for engineering courses.

There are many disciplines that can be taught using the robust and adaptable Raspberry Pi 5. It is an excellent approach to get youngsters interested in learning about science and technology.

Tips for utilising the Raspberry Pi 5 in the classroom

* Make use of an array of instructional resources. For the Raspberry Pi 5, there are numerous educational resources available, including books, online courses, and tutorials.

* Add some humour and interest. If students are enjoying themselves, they are more likely to learn. Aim to make your assignments and classes enjoyable and interesting for the pupils.

* Show patience. It takes time to learn. Allow your students to learn at their own pace and show them patience. Promote originality. The Raspberry Pi 5 is an excellent tool for artistic expression. Urge your pupils to be imaginative and to come up with their own initiatives.

Part 8: Robotics

Building robots using the Raspberry Pi 5

Robot construction is a nice use case for the Raspberry Pi 5. It is reasonably priced and powerful enough to perform a wide range of robotics applications.

You must install a robotics programme on your Raspberry Pi 5 before you can begin developing robots with it. Several common robotics applications are as follows:

* Python Robotics Library (PyRo)
* RobotJS
* Robot Operating System (ROS)
* Raspbian Robotics Toolkit

You must set up a robotics application to function with your robot hardware after installing it.

Depending on which robotics application you're using, the configuration procedure will change.

After configuring your robotics application, you are ready to begin developing your robot. A multitude of robot kits are available for use with the Raspberry Pi 5. You can also start from scratch and design your own robot.

Tips for using the Raspberry Pi 5 to construct robots:

* Begin with a basic project. Build a simple robot on your first attempt. Begin with a basic project, such building a robot with forward and backward motion. Employ a range of elements. The Raspberry Pi 5 can be used with a range of components, including motors, sensors, and actuators, to make robots. Try out various parts to determine which ones are most effective for your project.

* Seek out community assistance. Robot builders using Raspberry Pis are a sizable and vibrant

community. Never hesitate to ask for help from the community if you need it.

Installing and using robotics applications

You can follow the directions supplied by the programme developer to install a robotics application on the Raspberry Pi 5. The Raspberry Pi Package Manager may be used to install the majority of robotics software (apt).

The following command should be entered into a terminal window in order to install a robotics application using apt:

sudo apt install<application_name>

Put the name of the robotics application you wish to install in lieu of **<application_name>**

You may launch the robotics application by entering the following command in a terminal window after it has been installed:

application_name

Setting up your robot

After installing a robotics application on the Raspberry Pi 5, you must set it up to communicate with the hardware of your robot. Depending on which robotics application you're using, the configuration procedure will change. That being said, the majority of robotics software let you set up the following:

* Actuators, Motors, and Sensors

Follow the directions supplied by the robotics application developer to configure your robot.

Managing sensors and motors

Numerous GPIO pins on the Raspberry Pi 5 can be utilised to operate sensors and motors. A motor controller can be used with the Raspberry Pi 5 to control a motor. A circuit known as a motor controller transforms a low-voltage signal from the Raspberry Pi 5 into a high-voltage signal that is capable of powering a motor.

You can directly connect a sensor to the GPIO pins of the Raspberry Pi 5 in order to control it. Nevertheless, for certain sensors to function correctly, further circuitry is needed. To guarantee that it receives a steady voltage, for instance, a temperature sensor could need a voltage regulator.

Once your motors and sensors are connected to the Raspberry Pi 5, you can control them with a programming language like Python. The motor will run for ten seconds on this code, after which it will shut off. To adjust the motor's direction and speed, change the code.

The temperature will be read from the sensor by this code, which will then report it to the console. The code can be changed to send the temperature to a remote server or store it in a database.

Programming your robot

You may begin programming your robot once you understand how to use the Raspberry Pi 5 to operate motors and sensors. You can programme your robot using a number of different programming languages, including Python, Scratch, and C++.

Python is the recommended language to use if you are new to programming. Python is a rather simple language to learn, and getting started is made easier by the abundance of materials available.

You can use IDEs (Integrated Development Environments) like PyCharm and Visual Studio Code to programme your robot in Python. An IDE is a piece of software that offers a number of tools to make writing, running, and debugging code easier.

After selecting an IDE, you can begin programming your robot with code. To assist you in getting started, refer to the material in the preceding section.

You can use your Raspberry Pi 5 to control your robot once you've written some code. Debuggers can also be used to examine variable values and step through your code line by line.

Building a simple robot with the Raspberry Pi 5

With the Raspberry Pi 5, you'll need the following parts to make a basic robot:

* Hot glue gun
* Soldering iron (optional)
* Raspberry Pi 5
* Motor controller
* Motors (2)
* Wheels (2)
* Battery pack
* Jumper wires

* Breadboard

* Screws and nuts

You can begin constructing your robot as soon as you have assembled all of your parts. An outline of the procedure is given in the following steps:

1. Attach the motor controller to the Raspberry Pi 5. The GPIO pins on the Raspberry Pi 5 can be connected to the motor controller using jumper wires.

2. Attach the motor controller to the motors. Connecting the motors to the motor controller requires adhering to the manufacturer's instructions.

3. Fasten the motors to the wheels. To fasten the wheels to the motors, use nuts and screws.

4. Fasten the robot's battery pack to it. The battery pack and robot can be joined with hot glue.

5. If desired, solder the connectors connecting the motor controller to the motors. To strengthen the connections between the motor controller and the

motors, you can solder them if you have a soldering iron.

6. Setup the Raspberry Pi 5 with an application for robotics: To install the robotics application, according to the guidelines supplied by the developer.

7. Set up the robotics software to communicate with the hardware of your robot. To configure the programme, according to the guidelines supplied by the robotics application developer.

8. Set up your automaton. Your robot can be programmed using a programming language like Python.

After completing each of these processes, your robot will be prepared for use!

The robot will advance for ten seconds under this programming before coming to a stop. The robot's direction and speed can be adjusted by modifying the programming.

Sensors can also be used to increase the intelligence of your robot. For instance, you could programme your robot to avoid barriers by using a distance sensor.

Troubleshooting robotics problems

Check the connections. Verify that there are no loose connections amongst the motor controller, sensors, motors, and Raspberry Pi 5.

Examine the power source. Verify that the Raspberry Pi 5 and the motor controller are receiving enough electricity from the battery pack.

Verify the code. Verify that the code you are using is accurate and that it works with the robotics application you are using.

Verify the settings. Verify that the robotics application is compatible with your robot hardware and that it is configured correctly.

Verify the records. Error and warning logs may be retained by the robotics programme. Examine the logs to learn more about the issue.

Look up assistance online. You can solve robotics issues with the aid of a plethora of web resources.

Ask the community for assistance. Robot builders using Raspberry Pis are a sizable and vibrant community. Never hesitate to ask for help from the community if you need it.

Tips For common robotics issues

The robot is immobile. Verify that the motors are correctly linked to the motor controller. Verify that the Raspberry Pi 5 and motor controller are properly connected. Verify that there is adequate electricity going to the motor controller.

The robot has unpredictable movement. Verify that the motors are properly calibrated. Verify that the robot is standing on a level surface.

The robot is not obstacle aware. Verify that the distance sensor is properly attached to the

Raspberry Pi 5. Verify that the distance sensor is set up properly.

The robot has a crash. Verify that the code is accurate. Verify that the robot is not travelling too quickly. Verify that the robot is not attempting to navigate around obstructions.

If the issue persists after you have tried troubleshooting it, kindly share additional details about the problem, including the robotics application you are using, its version, the robot hardware you are using, and the troubleshooting steps you have already performed.

Part 9: Industrial Applications

Constructing Control Systems for Industry

One strong and adaptable platform for creating industrial control systems is the Raspberry Pi 5. It can run Linux and Windows among other operating systems, is quite cheap, and has a large number of GPIO pins.

In order to construct an industrial control system using the Raspberry Pi 5, the subsequent elements are required:

Industrial enclosure, Raspberry Pi 5; sensors, actuators; jumper wires; power supply; GPIO breakout board; optional DIN rail adapter

As soon as you have assembled every part, you may begin constructing your industrial control system. An outline of the procedure is given in the following steps:

1. Put the industrial enclosure together.
2. Attach the industrial enclosure and Raspberry Pi 5.
3. Attach the Raspberry Pi 5 to the power source.
4. Attach the Raspberry Pi to the GPIO breakout board. 5.
5. Attach the actuators and sensors to the breakout board of the GPIO.
6. Set up the Raspberry Pi 5's operating system and applications.
7. Evaluate the system of industrial control.

Building systems for data acquisition

Systems for acquiring data can also be made with the Raspberry Pi 5. Sensor data is gathered by data acquisition systems, which then transmit or store the data for additional analysis.

You'll need the following parts to build a Raspberry Pi 5 data collecting system:

An industrial enclosure, a Raspberry Pi 5, a power supply, a GPIO breakout board, sensors, jumper wires, a DIN rail adaptor (optional), and an SD card.

You can get started building your data gathering system as soon as you have assembled all of your parts. An outline of the procedure is given in the following steps:

1. Put the industrial enclosure together.
2. Attach the industrial enclosure and Raspberry Pi 5.
3. Attach the Raspberry Pi's power supply to it. 5.
4. Attach the Raspberry Pi to the GPIO breakout board. 5.
5. Attach the sensors to the breakout board of the GPIO.
6. Set up the Raspberry Pi 5's operating system and applications.

7. Write code to gather, store, and/or transmit data from the sensors.

8. Evaluate the mechanism for acquiring data.

Embedded systems using Raspberry Pi 5

Embedded systems can also make advantage of the Raspberry Pi 5. Computer systems called embedded systems are made to carry out particular functions inside of bigger systems.

You must install a light operating system, such as Raspbian Lite or Ubuntu Server, in order to use the Raspberry Pi 5 in an embedded system. Writing code is also required in order to programme the Raspberry Pi 5 to carry out the required functions.

Here are some instances of embedded systems that the Raspberry Pi 5 can be used to build:

* Media players

* Smart home appliances
* Industrial control systems
* Data collecting systems
* Robotics controllers

A multitude of embedded systems, data acquisition systems, and industrial control systems can be constructed using the flexible Raspberry Pi 5. It is a suitable option for a number of applications due to its large range of GPIO pins and relatively low cost.

Part 10: Advanced topics

Overclocking your Raspberry Pi 5

The act of raising a computer's CPU or GPU's clock speed is known as overclocking. The computer's performance may increase as a result, but it may also become less stable and use more power.

Your Raspberry Pi 5 can only be overclocked if you modify the `/boot/config.txt` file. The Raspberry Pi 5 setup settings, including the clock speed, are contained in this file.

With a text editor like nano or vi, you can alter the /boot/config.txt` file. After the file has been opened, locate the following lines:

arm_freq=2000
gpu_freq=1000

These lines provide the CPU and GPU clock speeds in MHz. In order to overclock your Raspberry Pi 5, you must raise these numbers.

It's crucial to remember that overclocking may reduce the stability of your Raspberry Pi 5. Your Raspberry Pi 5 can overheat or crash if you overclock it too much.

It's also crucial to remember that overclocking may cause your Raspberry Pi 5 to use more electricity. This implies that if you decide to overclock your Raspberry Pi 5, you might need to utilise a more potent power supply.

Utilising GPIO pins

Several GPIO pins on the Raspberry Pi 5 can be utilised to attach sensors and actuators. General-purpose input/output pins, or GPIO pins, are used for reading data from sensors and controlling devices.

In order to utilise the Raspberry Pi 5's GPIO pins, install the GPIO library for your preferred programming language. For instance, you can install the RPi.GPIO module if you're using Python.

After installing a GPIO library, you can use it to operate the Raspberry Pi 5's GPIO pins. For instance, the code provided will activate GPIO pin 18:

Additionally, GPIO pins can be used to read sensor data. To read the value of a temperature sensor connected to GPIO pin 17

Creating custom software

You can write bespoke software for a wide range of applications with the Raspberry Pi 5. You can write specialised software, for instance, for:

* Media players
* Smart home appliances
* Industrial control systems
* Data collecting systems
* Robotics controllers
* Security systems

The Raspberry Pi 5 requires you to select a development environment and a programming language in order to create custom applications. Python, C++, and Java are a few of the most popular programming languages for the Raspberry Pi 5.

Writing code to construct your own software can begin once you've selected a development environment and a programming language.

Dealing with complex issues

Many tools are available to assist you in troubleshooting complex issues if your Raspberry

Pi 5 isn't working properly. For instance, you can seek for assistance in the Raspberry Pi community or conduct a web search for it.

* Examine the logs. System events are recorded in logs by the Raspberry Pi 5. To learn more about the issue, review the logs.
* Employ a debugger. You can examine the values of variables and step through your code line by line with the aid of a debugger.
*Attempt an alternative operating system. Try another operating system, such Windows IoT Core or Ubuntu Server, if you are experiencing issues with your Raspberry Pi 5 running Raspbian.
*Seek assistance. A sizable and vibrant Raspberry Pi community exists. You can seek assistance in the Raspberry Pi community or online if you run into trouble.

Appendix

Raspberry Pi 5 GPIO pinout

The GPIO pins on the Raspberry Pi 5 are as follows:

Pin	Function
1	3.3V
2	5V
3	Ground
4	GPIO 2 (SDA)
5	GPIO 3 (SCL)
6	GPIO 4
7	GPIO 14 (TXD)
8	GPIO 15 (RXD)
9	Ground
10	GPIO 17 (SPI MOSI)
11	GPIO 18 (SPI MISO)
12	GPIO 27 (SPI CLK)
13	GPIO 22 (SPI CE1)

14	Ground
15	GPIO 23
16	GPIO 24
17	GPIO 25
18	GPIO 12
19	GPIO 16
20	GPIO 20
21	GPIO 21
22	Ground
23	GPIO 26
24	GPIO 19
25	GPIO 13
26	GPIO 6
27	Ground
28	GPIO 5
29	GPIO 4
30	ID SD
31	ID SC
32	Ground
33	PWM0
34	GPIO 11 (PWM1)

35	GPIO 9
36	GPIO 10
37	GPIO 8 (PWM0 ALT)
38	Ground
39	GPIO 7 (CE0)
40	GPIO 2 (SDA)

Raspberry Pi OS commands

* `sudo apt update && sudo apt upgrade`: Updates the software packages on your Raspberry Pi.

* `sudo apt install <package_name>`: Install a new software package on your Raspberry Pi.

* `sudo apt remove <package_name>`: Removes a software package from your Raspberry Pi.

* `sudo apt purge <package_name>`: Purges a software package from your Raspberry Pi and removes all of its associated configuration files.

* `sudo reboot`: Reboots your Raspberry Pi.

* `sudo halt`: Halts your Raspberry Pi.

Useful resources

Here are some useful resources for Raspberry Pi users:

* Raspberry Pi website: https://www.raspberrypi.org/
* Raspberry Pi documentation: https://www.raspberrypi.org/documentation/
* Raspberry Pi community forum: https://www.raspberrypi.org/forums/
* Raspberry Pi blog: https://www.raspberrypi.org/blog/

Made in the USA
Monee, IL
29 May 2024